First Edition

Disclaimer: The recipes and nutritional information in this book are provided for informational purposes only. The author and publisher are not liable for any adverse reactions, effects, or consequences resulting from the use of any recipes or suggestions herein.

Cover design by Fetch & Read
Food photography by Fetch & Read

Printed in the United States of America,
by www.ingramspark.com.

ISBN 979-8-9944325-2-5

www.FetchandRead.com

Fetch more tail wagging recipes
and pup-approved treats, visit

www.FetchandRead.com

INTRODUCTION

Every tail wag deserves a treat that's as wholesome as it is delicious! This cookbook was lovingly created to celebrate dogs who thrive on the power of plants. From crunchy veggies to juicy fruits and all-natural goodness in between.

Each recipe inside is crafted to be simple, nutritious, and tail-wag approved, focusing on ingredients that are gentle on the tummy and full of natural vitamins, minerals, and fiber. Whether your pup loves fresh snacks, cozy meals, or colorful treats, these recipes bring a paw-fect balance of flavor and nourishment to every bowl.

The Paw-fect Plant-Based Cookbook for Dogs was designed with pups of all kinds in mind. Including those with sensitive stomachs or special diets. You'll find vibrant, allergy-friendly creations that prove healthy eating can still be fun, flavorful, and full of love.

So grab your mixing bowl, roll up your sleeves, and get ready to cook up some plant powered joy. Every recipe is made with one simple goal in mind: to keep your best friend happy, healthy, and begging for seconds. Because when it comes to love, nothing says it better than a home-cooked paw-fectly plant-based meal.

Why Cook for Your Dog?

- 🐾 **Healthier Ingredients:**
  You control what goes into every bite—no hidden fillers or harmful additives.

- 🐾 **Tailored to Your Pup:**
  Recipes can be adjusted for your dog's size, preferences, or dietary needs.

- 🐾 **Bonding Time**
  Cooking for your dog is an act of love, and they'll feel it every time you share one of these homemade goodies.

- 🐾 **Cost-Effective**
  Many recipes use affordable, everyday ingredients—saving money compared to premium store-bought treats.

- 🐾 **Peace of Mind**
  You'll know exactly what your pup is eating, ensuring their snacks are both safe and delicious.

INGREDIENTS & BENEFITS

Blueberries	Blueberries are packed with antioxidants that help protect your dog's cells from damage, support brain health, and strengthen the immune system.
Bananas	Bananas provide a natural energy boost and are rich in potassium, which supports heart and muscle function while aiding digestion with gentle fiber.
Apples	Apples are full of vitamins A and C, help clean teeth naturally, and provide fiber that supports healthy digestion. Just remember to remove the seeds!
Pears	Pears are rich in fiber and vitamins C and K, helping with digestion and immune function while being gentle for dogs with sensitive stomachs.
Watermelon	Watermelon keeps dogs hydrated, offers a low-calorie snack option, and provides antioxidants like lycopene for heart and skin health.
Pineapple	Pineapple is a tropical treat high in vitamin C and manganese, and it contains bromelain, an enzyme that helps dogs digest proteins.
Papaya	Papaya supports digestion with natural enzymes, promotes healthy vision with vitamin A, and provides a sweet, low-fat source of fiber.
Unsweetened Applesauce	Unsweetened applesauce soothes the stomach, adds natural sweetness to recipes, and is rich in fiber and vitamin C.

INGREDIENTS & BENEFITS

Beets	Beets help boost stamina and detoxify the body thanks to their iron, potassium, and folate content, supporting blood and heart health.
Carrots	Carrots promote eye health and a strong immune system with beta-carotene, while also helping clean teeth naturally when eaten raw.
Cucumber	Cucumber is hydrating and low in calories, helping to keep dogs cool and refreshed while supporting skin and coat health.
Kale	Kale is packed with vitamins A, C, and K, promoting bone strength, immune support, and liver detoxification.
Zucchini	Zucchini provides hydration and gentle fiber to aid digestion while helping maintain a healthy weight.
Sweet Potato	Sweet potatoes are rich in fiber and beta-carotene, providing slow-release energy and promoting digestive health.
Green Beans	Green beans are an excellent source of fiber and vitamins A, C, and K, supporting healthy weight management and heart health.
Green Peas	Green peas are rich in plant protein and essential vitamins, helping with muscle development, energy, and digestion.
Spinach	Spinach delivers iron, antioxidants, and magnesium to support healthy blood circulation, muscle function, and a shiny coat.

INGREDIENTS & BENEFITS

Broccoli	Broccoli strengthens the immune system with vitamins C and K and supports healthy bones and digestion with fiber.
Red, Yellow, and Green Bell Peppers	Bell peppers are full of vitamin C and antioxidants that boost the immune system, protect vision, and add natural color and flavor to meals.
Parsnip	Parsnips contain potassium, folate, and fiber that help maintain heart health and support strong kidney function while adding natural sweetness.
Rolled Oats	Rolled oats provide gentle fiber for digestion, help maintain energy, and are rich in B vitamins that promote healthy skin and coat.
Oat Flour	Oat flour is a naturally gluten-free option that's easy to digest, providing healthy carbohydrates and fiber for sustained energy.
Chickpeas	Chickpeas are high in protein and fiber, supporting muscle repair, balanced energy, and digestive health.
Lentils	Lentils are rich in iron, folate, and fiber, promoting heart health, energy production, and regular digestion.
Brown Rice	Brown rice offers complex carbohydrates for steady energy and is easy to digest, providing essential minerals like magnesium and selenium.
Coconut Oil	Coconut oil supports a shiny coat, healthy skin, and boosts energy while providing antibacterial benefits through lauric acid.

INGREDIENTS & BENEFITS

Olive Oil	Olive oil delivers omega-3 fatty acids that reduce inflammation, promote heart health, and keep coats soft and glossy.
Ground Flaxseed	Ground flaxseed provides plant-based omega-3s that support digestion, reduce shedding, and nourish the skin and coat.
Pumpkin Purée	Pumpkin purée is high in fiber, helping regulate digestion while soothing upset stomachs and supporting a healthy immune system.
Vegetable Broth (Low Sodium)	Vegetable broth adds hydration and flavor to meals while encouraging picky eaters to enjoy nutritious veggies.

🐾 IMPORTANT DISCLAIMER & ALLERGY NOTICE

Foods to Avoid for Dogs:

While this cookbook focuses on safe, plant-based recipes, please never feed your dog the following foods:

- Grapes & Raisins
- Onions & Garlic
- Avocado
- Chocolate & Cocoa
- Caffeine (Coffee or Tea)
- Macadamia Nuts & Walnuts
- Xylitol (often found in sugar-free peanut butter or gum)
- Raw Dough or Yeast
- Unripe Tomatoes
- Excess Salt or Seasonings

Allergy Reminder:

Every dog is unique. Always introduce new foods slowly and in small amounts to ensure your pup doesn't have an allergic reaction or sensitivity.

If your dog has known allergies or a medical condition, consult your veterinarian before adding new ingredients to their diet.

RECIPES

🥕 Savory Meals & Stews
Green Goddess Pup Stew
Lentil & Pumpkin Pup Stew
Broccoli & Brown Rice Pup Casserole
Apple & Pumpkin Pup Porridge

🍠 Baked Treats & Chews
Sweet Potato & Apple Chew Sticks
Carrot & Chickpea Pup Patties
Pea & Pear Mash Cakes
Pear & Parsnip Biscuits
Zucchini Apple Mini Loaves
Apple Cinnamon Pup-Donuts

🍌 Fruity Snacks & Desserts
Blueberry Beet Balls
Banana Berry Pup Pizza
Tropical Pup Medley

🥗 Fresh Salads & Light Bites
Rainbow Pup Salad
Crispy Kale Pup Chips

GREEN GODDESS PUP STEW

A bright, nourishing stew packed with green veggies and gentle flavors — perfect for a healthy, happy pup!

INGREDIENTS

1 cup chopped spinach (fresh or frozen, thawed)
½ cup chopped zucchini
½ cup green beans, chopped
¼ cup peas (fresh or frozen)
½ pear, peeled and finely diced (adds gentle sweetness)
1 ½ cups water or low-sodium vegetable broth
1 tsp coconut oil (optional, for shine and healthy fats)

INSTRUCTIONS

1. In a medium saucepan, add coconut oil and lightly sauté zucchini, green beans, and peas for 2–3 minutes.
2. Add water (or broth) and bring to a gentle simmer.
3. Stir in chopped spinach and diced pear.
4. Simmer on low for 10 minutes until vegetables are soft.
5. Remove from heat and let cool completely before serving.

LENTIL & PUMPKIN PUP STEW

A warm, comforting stew packed with plant--based protein, fiber, and vitamins.

INGREDIENTS

1 cup cooked lentils (green or brown, unsalted)
½ cup pumpkin purée (unsweetened, 100% pumpkin)
½ cup diced carrots
¼ cup chopped greeen beans
¼ cup peas (fresh or frozen)
2 cups water or low-sodium vegetable broth
1 tsp coconut oil (optional, for shine and coat health)

INSTRUCTIONS

1. In a medium pot, heat coconut oil over low heat (optional).

2. Add carrots, peas, and green beans. Sauté for 3–4 minutes until slightly tender.

3. Stir in cooked lentils and pumpkin purée.

4. Add water or vegetable broth and bring to a gentle simmer.

5. Cook for 10–12 minutes, stirring occasionally, until vegetables are soft and stew thickens.

BROCCOLI & BROWN RICE PUP CASSEROLE

A cozy, oven-baked casserole made with nourishing brown rice, broccoli, and peas—perfect for a satisfying dinner for your pup!

INGREDIENTS

1 cup cooked brown rice
½ cup finely chopped broccoli
(steamed or lightly cooked)
¼ cup peas (fresh or frozen)
¼ cup grated carrots
¼ cup pumpkin puree
(for moisture and sweetness)
1 tbsp ground flaxseed
(for fiber and binding)
1 tsp coconut oil
(optional, for shine
and coat health)

INSTRUCTIONS

1. Preheat oven to 350°F (175°C).
2. In a large bowl, combine cooked brown rice, broccoli, peas, carrots, pumpkin puree, and flaxseed.
3. Mix well until the ingredients are evenly coated and hold together slightly.
4. Transfer mixture into a small, greased baking dish or silicone mold.
5. Bake for 20-25 minutes, until the top is firm and slightly golden.
6. Allow to cool completely before serving to your pup.

🐾 **Paw-fect Tip** This casserole freezes well!

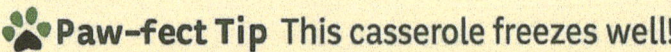

APPLE & PUMPKIN PUP PORRIDGE

A warm, comforting porridge that's sweet, smooth, and packed with fiber – perfect for pups who love cozy meals!

INGREDIENTS

½ cup rolled oats
1 cup water (or unsalted vegetable broth)
½ cup unsweetened pumpkin purée
½ apple (peeled and finely chopped or grated)
1 tsp ground flaxseed (optional, for fiber)
1 tsp coconut oil (optional, for coat health)
Pinch of dog-safe cinnamon (optional, for aroma)

INSTRUCTIONS

1. In a small saucepan, bring water (or broth) to a gentle boil.
2. Add oats and cook for 5–7 minutes, stirring occasionally until soft.
3. Stir in pumpkin purée, chopped apple, flaxseed, and cinnamon.
4. Cook for another 2–3 minutes until the mixture thickens into a porridge.
5. Remove from heat, stir in coconut oil, and let cool to a safe serving temperature.

 **Paw-fect Tip**

Serve warm for breakfast or refrigerate for a chilled, pudding-style snack.

You can top it with a few fresh apple bits for extra crunch!

SWEET POTATO & APPLE CHEW STICKS

INGREDIENTS

1 cup cooked sweet potato, mashed

1 small apple, peeled and finely grated

1 cup oat flour (or finaily ground rolled oats)

1 tbsp coconut oil (optional, for texture)

2 tbsp water (adjust as needed)

INSTRUCTIONS

1. Preheat oven to 325°F (160°C).
2. In a large bowl, combine mashed sweet potato, grated apple, and coconut oil.
3. Stir in oat flour and gradually add water until a soft dough forms.
4. Roll dough into long stick shapes about the thickness of a(pencil).
6. Bake for 25-30 minutes, until firm and lightly golden.
7. Allow to cool completely.

PAW-FECT TIP

For extra chewy texture, store in the fridge overnight.

CARROT & CHICKPEA PUP PATTIES

Golden, protein-packed patties made with chickpeas and sweet carrots—perfect for lunch or dinner for your veggie-loving pup!

INGREDIENTS

1 cup cooked chickpeas (mashed or lightly blended)
½ cup grated carrots
¼ cup mashed sweet potato (optional for softness)
1 tbsp ground flaxseed (for binding)
½ cup oat flour (or finely ground rolled oats)
1 tbsp coconut oil (optional, for a golden finish)
2 tbsp water (adjust for texture)

INSTRUCTIONS

1. Preheat oven to 350°F (175°C).

2. In a large bowl, combine mashed chickpeas, grated carrots, sweet potato, and flaxseed.

3. Stir in oat flour and add water gradually until the mixture holds together.

4. Shape the mixture into small, round patties (about 2 inches wide).

5. Place on a parchment-lined baking sheet and brush lightly with coconut oil.

6. Bake for 25–30 minutes, flipping halfway through for even browning.

7. Let cool completely before serving to your pup.

PEA & PEAR MASH CAKES

INGREDIENTS

- 1 cup green peas (fresh or thawed from frozen)
- 1 ripe pear, peeled and finely grated
- 1 cup oat flour (or finely ground rolled oats)
- 1 tbsp coconut oil (optional, for texture)
- 2 tbsp water (adjust for consistency

INSTRUCTIONS

1. Preheat oven to 350°F (175°C).
2. Steam or microwave peas until soft, then mash or pulse in a blender.
3. In a bowl, combine mashed peas, grated pear, oat flour, and coconut oil.
4. Add water a little at a time until the mixture forms a soft dough.
5. Scoop small spoonfuls and shape into mini cakes or patties.
6. Place on a parchment-lined baking sheet.
7. Bake for 20–25 minutes, until lightly golden and firm.
8. Let cool completely before serving.

PAW-FECT TIP Serve warm for a soft texture or refrigerate for a firmer, chewier treat.

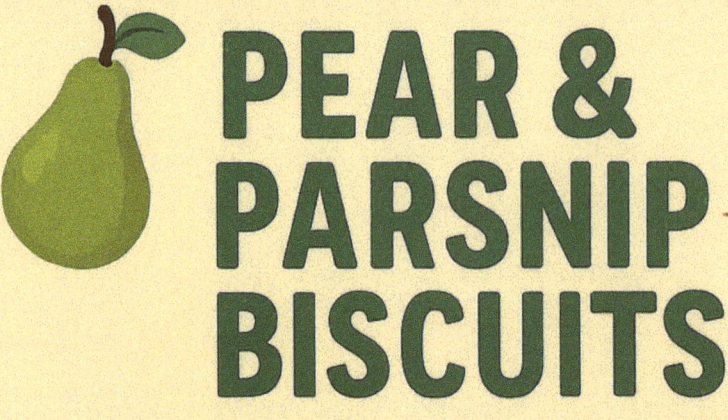

PEAR & PARSNIP BISCUITS

A lightly sweet, soft-baked treat made with fresh pears and parsnips—perfect for pups who love fruity and earthy flavors!

Ingredients

1 cup pear, peeled and grated (ripe but firm)

½ cup parsnip, peeled and grated

1 cup oat flour (or finely ground rolled oats)

1 tbsp coconut oil (optional, helps with texture)

¼ cup water (adjust as needed)

Instructions

1. Preheat oven to 325°F (160°C).
2. Peel and grate pear and parsnip. Pat pear with a paper towel to remove excess moisture.
3. In a bowl, combine grated pear, parsnip, oat flour, and coconut oil.
4. Add water gradually until dough holds together.
5. Roll out dough on a floured surface to about ¼ inch thick.
6. Cut into fun shapes with cookie cutters (bones, paws, hearts).
7. Place biscuits on a parchment-lined baking sheet.
8. Cool completely before serving.

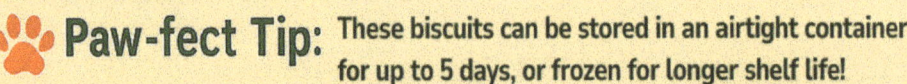 **Paw-fect Tip:** These biscuits can be stored in an airtight container for up to 5 days, or frozen for longer shelf life!

ZUCCHINI APPLE MINI LOAVES

🐾 Paw-fect Tip

Slice loaves into small bite-sized pieces for training treats, or serve as a special snack! Store in an airtight container for up to 4 days, or freeze for longer freshness.

INGREDIENTS

- 1 cup zucchini, finely grated (pat dry with a paper
- 1 cup apple, peeled and grated
- 1½ cups oat flour (or finely ground rolled oats)
- 1 tsp cinnarnon (optional, dog-safe in small amounts)
- 1 tbsp coconut oil (optional, for moisture)
- ½ cup water (adjust as needed)

INSTRUCTIONS

1. Preheat oven to 350°F (175°C)
2. Grate zucchini and apple, then pat dry to remove excess moisture.
3. In a large bowl, combine oat flour, zucchini, apple cinnamon, and coconut oil.
4. Slowly add water until mixture forms a thick batter.
5. Pour batter into lightly greased mini loaf pans or silicone molds.
6. Bake for 20-25 minutes, or until a toothpick comes out clean.
7. Allow to cool completely before serving.

Apple Cinnamon Pup-donuts

Soft, baked mini donuts made with fresh apple and a hint of dog-safe cinnamon—a cozy treat pup!

Ingredients

1 cup oat flour (or finely ground rolled oats)

½ cup unsweetened applesauce (or pureed apple)

1 small apple, peeled and finely grated

1 tsp cinnamon (dog-safe in small amounts)

1 tbsp coconut oil (optional, for moisture)

¼ cup water (adjust as needed)

Instructions

1. Preheat oven to 350°F (175*C).
2. In a bowl, combine oat flour, cinnamon, applesauce, and grated apple.
3. Stir in coconut oil and water gradually until batter is thick but pourable.
4. Spoon or pipe the batter into a greased mini donut pan.
5. Bake for 15-18 minutes, until goiden and firm.
6. Allow to cool completely before serving.

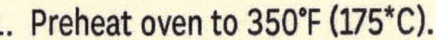

🐾 Paw-fect Tip

For an extra fun touch, dip the cooled donuts in unsweetened coconut yogurt and sprinkle with a few finely shredded carrots

BLUEBERRY BEET BALLS

Colorful, bite-sized energy balls packed with **antioxidant** fiber—a sweet and earthy treat for your pup!

INGREDIENTS

½ cup blueberries (fresh or frozen, unsweetened)

½ cup cooked beets (peeled and finely grated or mashed)

1 ripe banana, mashed

1 cup rolled oats

INSTRUCTIONS

1. Mash banana in a large bowl until smooth.
2. Add grated beet and blueberries, mixing gently to combine.
3. Stir in oats until mixture becomes sticky and dough-like.
4. Roll into small bite—sized balls (about 1 inch).
5. Place on a parchment-lined tray and refrigerate for 2-3 hours until firm.

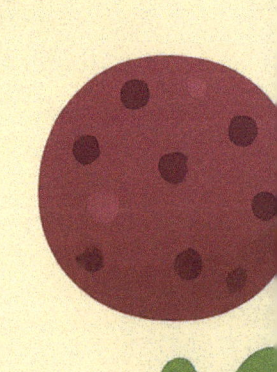

BANANA BERRY PUP PIZZA

A sweet, colorful treat with a soft oat crust, creamy banana base, and juicy berry toppings — perfect for snack time

INGREDIENTS:

For the Crust:

1 cup oat flour
   (or finely ground rolled oats)
1 ripe banana, mashed
2 tbsp unsweetened applesauce
1 tbsp coconut oil
   (optional, for moisture)

For the Toppings:

½ banana, sliced
⅓ cup blueberries
¼ cup diced strawberries

INSTRUCTIONS:

1. Preheat oven to 350°F (175°C).
2. In a bowl, mix oat flour, mashed banana, applesauce, and coconut oil to form a soft dough.
3. Roll out dough into a small circle (about ¼-inch thick) and place on parchment paper.
4. Bake for 15–20 minutes, until firm but not too crisp.
5. Let cool completely.
6. Spread a thin layer of unsweetened coconut yogurt over the crust (optional).
7. Arrange banana slices, strawberries, and blueberries on top like a colorful pizza.

TROPICAL PUP MEDLEY

A refreshing mix of tropical fruits – juicy, sweet, and paw-fect for pups who love a fruit treat!

INGREDIENTS

½ cup pineapple (small pieces, core removed)

½ cup papaya, cubed

1 ripe banana, sliced

½ cup seedless watermelon, cubed

½ cup blueberries

INSTRUCTIONS

1. Wash and prepare all fruits (remove seeds, skins, and cores where needed).

2. Cut pineapple, papaya, banana, and watermelon into bite-sized cubes.

3. Add all fruits to a bowl and toss gently to combine.

🐾 **Paw-fect Tip:** Freeze the fruit mix in silicone molds for a cold, hydrating summer treat!

RAINBOW PUP SALAD

A colorful, crunchy mix of fruits and veggies that's as fun as it is healthy for your pup!

Ingredients:

½ cup cucumber, chopped

½ cup carrots, shredded

½ cup bell peppers
(red, yellow, green), chopped

½ cup blueberries

½ cup watermelon, cubed
(seedless)

Instructions

1. Wash all fruits and veggies thoroughly.
2. Chop cucumber, peppers, and watermelon into bite-sized cubes.
3. Shred carrots for extra crunch
4. Add everything to a bowl, tossing lightly to combine.
5. Serve fresh in small portions as a snack or meal topper.

 Paw-fect Tip: Switch up the ingredients with other dog-safe fruits and veggies (like apples,

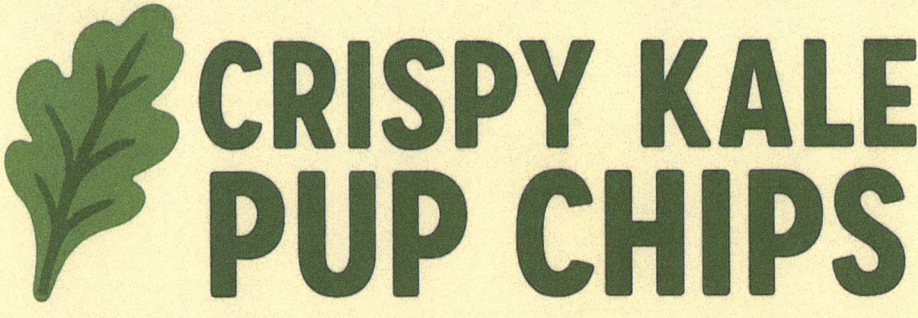

CRISPY KALE PUP CHIPS

A light, crunchy green treat that's packed with vitamins and a satisfying crunch for your pup!

Ingredients:

2 cups fresh kale leaves (washed, stems removed, torn into bite-sized pieces)

1 tsp olive oil (optional, light coating)

Instructions

Paw-fect Tip:
Let it cool before serving.

1. Preheat oven to 250°F (120°C).
2. Wash kale thoroughly and pat dry with a paper towel.
3. Remove tough stems and tear leaves into small, pup-sized pieces.
4. (Optional) Toss kale lightly in olive oil for extra crispness.
5. Spread kale evenly on a parchment-lined baking sheet.
6. Bake for 25-30 minutes, flipping halfway through, until crispy.

Thank You

From the bottom of my heart, thank you for joining me on this journey and for choosing to share these recipes with your pup.

Every recipe in this book was created with love, with the hope that each tail wag, happy bark, and eager lick reminds you of the joy our dogs bring into our lives. They are more than pets, they are family.

By taking the time to make healthy, homemade treats, you're giving your dog more than just food:

You're giving them wellness, by nourishing their bodies with safe, wholesome ingredients.

You're giving them happiness, because good food lifts their mood, brightens their spirit, and fills their day with joy.

Most importantly, you're giving them love. The kind they'll return endlessly, in every cuddle, every wag, and every look that says, "You are my favorite person."

This book isn't just about recipes. It's about deepening the bond between you and your best friend. Healthy treats and meals are one of the many ways to say, "I love you." And dogs, with their big hearts and loyal souls, will love you back a thousand times more for it.

So here's to you, your pup, and the countless moments of happiness these recipes will bring. May every bite remind you of the incredible gift we have in our dogs—unconditional love.

www.ingramcontent.com/pod-product-compliance
Lightning Source LLC
Chambersburg PA
CBHW051601120626
46551CB00013B/1619